"9Marks, as a ministry, has taken basic biblical tea[...] the hands of pastors. Bobby, by way of these stud[...] delivered it to the person in the pew. I am unawa[...] and practically helps Christians understand God'[...] to use these studies in my own congregation."

D0128988

    Jeramie Rinne, Senior Pastor, South Shore Baptist Church, Hingham, Massachusetts

"Bobby Jamieson has done local church pastors an incredible service by writing these study guides. Clear, biblical, and practical, they introduce the biblical basis for a healthy church. But more importantly, they challenge and equip church members to be part of the process of improving their own church's health. The studies work for individual, small group, and larger group settings. I have used them for the last year at my own church and appreciate how easy they are to adapt to my own setting. I don't know of anything else like them. Highly recommended!"

    Michael Lawrence, Senior Pastor, Hinson Baptist Church, *Biblical Theology in the Life of the Church*

"This is a Bible study that is actually rooted in the Bible and involves actual study. In the 9Marks Healthy Church Study Guides series a new standard has been set for personal theological discovery and corresponding personal application. Rich exposition, compelling questions, and clear syntheses combine to give a guided tour of ecclesiology—the theology of the church. I know of no better curriculum for generating understanding of and involvement in the church than this. It will be a welcome resource in our church for years to come."

    Rick Holland, Senior Pastor, Mission Road Bible Church, Prairie Village, Kansas

"In America today we have the largest churches in the history of our nation, but the least amount of impact for Christ's kingdom. Slick marketing and finely polished vision statements are a foundation of sand. The 9Marks Healthy Church Study Guides series is a refreshing departure from church-growth materials, towards an in-depth study of God's Word that will equip God's people with his vision for his Church. These study guides will lead local congregations to abandon secular methodologies for church growth and instead rely on Christ's principles for developing healthy, God-honoring assemblies."

    Carl J. Broggi, Senior Pastor, Community Bible Church, Beaufort, South Carolina; President, Search the Scriptures Radio Ministry

"Anyone who loves Jesus will love what Jesus loves. The Bible clearly teaches that Jesus loves the church. He knows about and cares for individual churches and wants them to be spiritually healthy and vibrant. Not only has Jesus laid down his life for the church but he has also given many instructions in his Word regarding how churches are to live and function in the world. This series of Bible studies by 9Marks shows how Scripture teaches these things. Any Christian who works through this curriculum, preferably with other believers, will be helped to see in fresh ways the wisdom, love, and power of God in establishing the church on earth. These studies are biblical, practical, and accessible. I highly recommend this curriculum as a useful tool that will help any church embrace its calling to display the glory of God to a watching world."

    Thomas Ascol, Senior Pastor, Grace Baptist Church of Cape Coral, Florida; Executive Director, Founders Ministries

9MARKS HEALTHY CHURCH STUDY GUIDES

Built upon the Rock: The Church

Hearing God's Word: Expositional Preaching

The Whole Truth about God: Biblical Theology

God's Good News: The Gospel

Real Change: Conversion

Reaching the Lost: Evangelism

Committing to One Another: Church Membership

Guarding One Another: Church Discipline

Growing One Another: Discipleship in the Church

Leading One Another: Church Leadership

GUARDING ONE ANOTHER: CHURCH DISCIPLINE

Bobby Jamieson
Mark Dever, General Editor
Jonathan Leeman, Managing Editor

HEALTHY CHURCH STUDY GUIDES

WHEATON, ILLINOIS

Guarding One Another: Church Discipline

Copyright © 2012 by 9Marks

Published by Crossway
    1300 Crescent Street
    Wheaton, Illinois 60187

Cover design: Dual Identity inc.

First printing 2012

Printed in the United States of America

Trade paperback ISBN: 978-1-4335-2552-0

PDF ISBN: 978-1-4335-2553-7

Mobipocket ISBN: 978-1-4335-2554-4

ePub ISBN: 978-1-4335-2555-1

Crossway is a publishing ministry of Good News Publishers.

LB		20	19	18	17	16	15	14	13	12
15	14	13	12	11	10	9	8	7	6	5	4	3	2	1

CONTENTS

Introduction   7

An Important Mark of a Healthy Church:
Biblical Church Discipline, *by Mark Dever*   11

Week 1
Is Discipline Loving?   17

Week 2
Formative Discipline: Building Up the Church   21

Week 3
Dealing with Sin, Part 1   25

Week 4
Dealing with Sin, Part 2   29

Week 5
Dealing with Sin, Part 3   33

Week 6
Repentance and Restoration   37

Teacher's Notes   41

INTRODUCTION

What does the local church mean to you?

Maybe you love your church. You love the people. You love the preaching, the singing. You can't wait to show up on Sunday, and you cherish fellowship with other church members throughout the week.

Maybe the church is just a place you show up to a couple times a month. You sneak in late, duck out early.

We at 9Marks are convinced that the local church is God's plan for displaying his glory to the nations. And we want to help you catch and live out that vision, together with your whole church.

The 9Marks Healthy Church Study Guides are a series of six- or seven-week studies on each of the "nine marks of a healthy church" plus one introductory study. These nine marks are the core convictions of our ministry. To provide a quick introduction to them, we've included a chapter from Mark Dever's book *What Is a Healthy Church?* with each study. We don't claim that these nine marks are the most important things about the church or the only important things about the church. But we do believe that they are biblical and therefore are helpful for churches.

So, in these studies, we're going to work through the biblical foundations and practical applications of each one. The ten studies are:

- *Built upon the Rock: The Church* (the introductory study)
- *Hearing God's Word: Expositional Preaching*
- *The Whole Truth about God: Biblical Theology*
- *God's Good News: The Gospel*
- *Real Change: Conversion*
- *Reaching the Lost: Evangelism*
- *Committing to One Another: Church Membership*

- *Guarding One Another: Church Discipline*
- *Growing One Another: Discipleship in the Church*
- *Leading One Another: Church Leadership*

Each session of these studies takes a close look at one or more passages of Scripture and considers how it applies to the life of the whole church. So, we hope that these studies are equally appropriate for Sunday school, small groups, and other contexts where a group of anywhere from two to two-hundred people can come together and discuss God's Word.

These studies are mainly driven by observation, interpretation, and application questions, so get ready to speak up! We also hope that these studies provide opportunities for people to reflect together on their experiences in the church, whatever those experiences may be.

If you want to be physically healthy, you need rest, a good diet, and regular exercise. You may need to cultivate some good habits and cut off some bad ones.

If you want to learn a foreign language you have to memorize vocabulary and verb forms and practice speaking it until it feels like your head is going to fall off. And you also have to be willing to constantly receive correction to bring your pronunciation closer and closer to the mark.

If you want to be a champion swimmer you have to not only practice and train but also receive your coach's correction so that your stroke becomes more efficient.

From all of these things and more, it's obvious that we need discipline. Discipline is both positive and negative, practice and correction, learning and unlearning.

In a church, discipline is no different. In order to grow to maturity in Christ we need teaching and encouragement, and we also need correction. We need people to spur us on, and we need people to turn us around when we're heading in the wrong direction.

Church discipline encompasses all of this: encouraging and correcting, teaching and confronting.

This study on church discipline begins by addressing the most common objection to it: "That's not loving!" Next, we consider how to build one another up in the church (what theologians call "formative discipline"). The next three studies all examine New Testament passages that teach us how to deal with sin in the local church (what theologians call "corrective discipline"). Finally, we study repentance and restoration, which is the goal corrective discipline aims for.

Like an hour at the gym or a full day of speaking a new language, discipline hurts. But it's a pain that brings growth and strength in its wake. So let's find out what growth and strength God will give us as we apply ourselves to his discipline in the church.

AN IMPORTANT MARK OF A HEALTHY CHURCH: BIBLICAL CHURCH DISCIPLINE

BY MARK DEVER

(Adapted from chapter 11 of What Is a Healthy Church?*)*

Biblical church discipline flows directly out of a biblical understanding of church membership. Membership draws a boundary line around the church, marking the church off from the world. Discipline helps the church that lives inside of that boundary line stay true to the very things that are cause for drawing the line in the first place. It gives meaning to being a member of the church and is another important mark of a healthy church.

What exactly is church discipline? In a broad sense, discipline is teaching. In a more narrow sense, some discipline is corrective. In the narrowest sense, it is the act of excluding someone who professes to be a Christian from membership in the church and participation in the Lord's Supper for serious unrepentant sin—sin they refuse to let go of.

IMAGING GOD'S CHARACTER

In order to understand church discipline, it might help us to remind ourselves of God's purposes in creating the universe, humanity, Israel, and the church. God created the universe in order to display his glory. He then created humanity for the same purpose, and particularly by creating us to bear his image (Gen. 1:27). Humanity—Adam and Eve—didn't display his glory, so he excluded them from the garden.

God then called Israel to display his glory, particularly by displaying his holiness and character to the nations as they were revealed in the law (see Lev. 19:2; Prov. 24:1, 25). Along the way, this law was the basis for correcting and even excluding some people from the community (as in Num. 15:30–31). Ultimately, it was the basis for excluding Israel itself from the land.

Finally, God created the church, we have said, so that it might increasingly reflect the character of God as it's been revealed in his Word. In keeping with the storyline of the entire Bible, then, church discipline is the act of excluding an individual who carelessly brings disrepute onto the gospel and shows no commitment to doing otherwise. Discipline helps the church to reflect God's glorious character faithfully. It helps the church to remain holy. It's an attempt to polish the mirror and remove any specks (see 2 Cor. 6:14–7:1; 13:2; 1 Tim. 6:3–5; 2 Tim. 3:1–5). Why discipline? So that the holy and loving character of God might appear more clearly and shine more brightly.

HOW DOES IT WORK?

How does the process of discipline work? Since the circumstances of sin vary tremendously, so does the need for pastoral wisdom in knowing how to treat each situation particularly.

That said, Jesus's words in Matthew 18 provide the general boundaries (Matt. 18:15–17). Begin by addressing a sinning brother or sister in private. If the sinner repents, the process of discipline ends. If not, then return a second time with another Christian. If he or she still doesn't repent, then, as Jesus put it, "tell it to the church; and if they refuse to listen even to the church, treat them as you would a pagan or a tax collector" (Matt. 18:17 NIV), that is, like an outsider.

SHALT THOU JUDGE?

This whole idea can sound harsh to many people today. Besides, didn't Jesus forbid his followers from judging others? In one sense, he certainly did: "Do not judge, or you too will be judged" (Matt. 7:1 NIV). But in the very same Gospel, Jesus also called churches to rebuke—even publicly—their members for sin (Matt. 18:15–17; cf. Luke 17:3). So whatever Jesus meant by "Do not judge," he did not mean to rule out everything that might be called "judging" today.

Certainly God himself is a judge. He judged Adam in the garden. In the Old Testament he judged both nations and individuals. In the New Testament he promises that Christians will be judged according to their works (see 1 Corinthians 3). And he promises that, on the final day, he will reveal himself as the ultimate judge of all humanity (see Revelation 20).

In his judgment, God is never wrong. He is always righteous (see Joshua 7; Matthew 23; Luke 2; Acts 5; Romans 9). Sometimes his purposes in judgment are corrective, redemptive, and restorative, as when he disciplines his children. Sometimes his purposes are retributive, vengeful, and final, as when he bears his wrath upon the ungodly (see Hebrews 12). Either way, God's judgment is always just.

What may surprise many people today is that God occasionally uses human beings to carry out his judgment. The state is given responsibility to judge its citizens (see Romans 13). Christians are told to judge themselves (see 1 Cor. 11:28; Hebrews 4; 2 Pet. 1:5). Congregations are told to occasionally even judge the members of the church—though not in the final way God judges.

In Matthew 18, 1 Corinthians 5 and 6, and elsewhere, the church is instructed to exercise judgment within itself. This judgment is for redemptive, not vengeful, purposes (Rom. 12:19). Paul told the church in Corinth to hand the adulterous man over to Satan "so that [the sinful nature may be destroyed and] his spirit may be saved" (1 Cor. 5:5 NIV). He says the same to Timothy regarding the false teachers in Ephesus (1 Tim. 1:20).

CLOSED OR OPEN?

We should not be surprised that God calls us to exercise certain forms of judgment or discipline. If churches expect to have anything to say about how Christians do live, they will have to say something about how Christians do not live. Yet I worry that the way many churches approach discipleship is like pouring water into leaking buckets—all the attention is given to what is poured in with no thought given to how it's received and kept. One sign of this tendency is the decline in the practice of church discipline in the last few generations.

One church-growth writer recently summed up his strategy on growing churches by saying, "Open the front door and close the back door." By this he means that churches should make themselves more accessible to outsiders while also doing a better job of follow-up. These are good goals. Yet I suspect that most pastors and churches today already aspire to do this, and to a fault. So let me offer what I believe is a more biblical strategy: guard carefully the front door and open the back door. In other words, make it more difficult to join, on the one hand, and make it easier to be excluded on the other. Remember—the path to life is narrow, not broad. Doing this, I believe, will help churches to recover their divinely intended distinction from the world.

One of the first steps in exercising discipline, therefore, is to exercise greater care in receiving new members. A church should ask every individual applying for membership what the gospel is and ask each one to give some evidence of understanding the nature of a Christ-honoring life. Member candidates will benefit from knowing what the church expects from them and the importance of commitment. If churches are more careful about recognizing and receiving new members, they will have less occasion to practice corrective church discipline later.

DOING DISCIPLINE RESPONSIBLY

Church discipline can be done badly. The New Testament teaches us not to judge others for the motives we might impute to them (see Matt. 7:1), or to judge each other about matters that are not essential (see Romans 14–15). In carrying out discipline, our attitudes must not be vindictive but loving, demonstrating a "mercy, mixed with fear" (Jude 23 NIV). There's no denying it, church discipline is fraught with problems of wisdom and pastoral application. But we must remember that the whole Christian life is difficult and open to abuse. And our difficulties should not be used as an excuse to leave something unpracticed.

Each local church has a responsibility to judge the life and teaching of its leaders and members, particularly when either compromises the church's witness to the gospel (see Acts 17; 1 Corinthians 5; 1 Timothy 3; James 3:1; 2 Peter 3; 2 John).

Biblical church discipline is simple obedience to God and a confession that we need help. Can you imagine a world in which God never used our fellow human beings to enact his judgment, one in which parents never disciplined children, the state never punished lawbreakers, and churches never reproved their members? We would all arrive at judgment day never having felt the lash of earthly judgment and so been forewarned of the greater judgment then upon us. How merciful of God to teach us now about the irrevocable justice to come with these temporary chastisements (see Luke 12:4–5).

Here are five positive reasons for practicing corrective church discipline. It shows love for:

1) the good of the disciplined individual;
2) other Christians as they see the danger of sin;
3) the health of the church as a whole;
4) the corporate witness of the church and, therefore, non-Christians in the community; and
5) the glory of God.

Our holiness should reflect God's holiness. It should mean something to be a member of the church, not for our pride's sake, but for God's name's sake. Biblical church discipline is another important mark of a healthy church.

WEEK 1
IS DISCIPLINE LOVING?

GETTING STARTED

1. What is the first thing that comes to mind when you hear the word "discipline"?

2. What other things do you associate with the idea of discipline? Are these things good or bad? Pleasant or unpleasant?

This lesson begins a series of six studies on the topic of church discipline. Since this is a neglected and challenging topic, let's begin with some basic teaching before jumping into the Bible passage we're going to focus on.

Defining Discipline
Broadly speaking, *discipline* is everything the church does to help its members pursue holiness and fight sin. Preaching, teaching, prayer, reading and memorizing the Bible, corporate worship, accountability relationships, and godly oversight by pastors and elders are all forms of discipline. Theologians often call this kind of discipline "formative discipline" because it forms our character to be more like Christ.

In a narrower sense, discipline is when we point out fellow church members' sin and encourage them to repent and pursue holiness by God's grace. Theologians often call this kind of discipline "corrective discipline." It means correcting fellow church members when they begin to veer from the path of following Christ. As we'll see in coming studies, Jesus commands the church not only to correct sin and pursue the sinner's repentance but also to exclude someone from the church if they continue to cling to their sin instead of clinging to Jesus.

Is Discipline Loving?

Discipline involves correction, confrontation, and, if necessary, exclusion. When some people hear this, they throw up their hands and say, "I want nothing to do with that! That's the most unloving thing I've ever heard!"

Thus, this study answers the question: Is discipline loving? In order to do that, we're going to consider a passage of Scripture that teaches us about how God disciplines us and why.

MAIN IDEA

God disciplines us because he loves us. His purpose is to help his children grow in holiness and humble dependence on him.

DIGGING IN

The book of Hebrews is filled with stirring exhortations to keep on trusting in Christ through opposition, persecution, and suffering. In this study we'll consider Hebrews 12:3–11:

> [3] Consider him who endured from sinners such hostility against himself, so that you may not grow weary or fainthearted. [4] In your struggle against sin you have not yet resisted to the point of shedding your blood. [5] And have you forgotten the exhortation that addresses you as sons?
>
> > "My son, do not regard lightly the discipline of the Lord,
> >   nor be weary when reproved by him.
> > [6] For the Lord disciplines the one he loves,
> >   and chastises every son whom he receives."
>
> [7] It is for discipline that you have to endure. God is treating you as sons. For what son is there whom his father does not discipline? [8] If you are left without discipline, in which all have participated, then you are illegitimate children and not sons. [9] Besides this, we have had earthly fathers who disciplined us and we respected them. Shall we not much more be subject to the Father of spirits and live? [10] For they disciplined us for a short time as it seemed best to them, but he disciplines us for our good, that we may share his holiness. [11] For the moment all discipline seems painful rather than pleasant, but later it yields the peaceful fruit of righteousness to those who have been trained by it.

1. *In verse three, what does the author of Hebrews exhort us to do? For what purpose?*

2. *According to verses 5 and 6, whom does God discipline? What does this teach us about God's attitude toward those whom he disciplines?*

3. *Many people have had human fathers who disciplined them in anger, in self-ishness, and in excess. What can we be certain about when it comes to God's discipline?*

4. *What does the "exhortation that addresses you as sons" (Prov. 3:11–12) tell us to do? Why (Heb. 12:5–6)?*

5. *Put yourself in the shoes of believers who are being persecuted and harassed for their faith. Why is it especially comforting to know that you are God's child, and that these circumstances, among other purposes, may be his way of disciplining and teaching you?*

6. *What comparison do verses 7 through 11 draw? How does this help us to understand God's discipline?*

7. *What does verse 8 say about those who have not received God's discipline? How should this comfort us when we do receive God's discipline?*

8. *What is the proper response to parental discipline (v. 9)?*

9. *According to verse 10, our earthly fathers disciplined us*

- _____ a _____ _____
- as it _____ best _____ _____.

But God disciplines us:

- _____ _____ _____
- that we may _____ _____ _____.

What does this comparison teach us about how we should respond to God's discipline?

10. *What does discipline feel like* now? *What does it bring about later (v. 11)? Give some concrete examples of situations in which this long-term perspective can help us endure God's discipline.*

Looking back over the whole passage, we see that it teaches us several things about God's discipline:

- The *objects* of God's discipline are his children (vv. 5–8).
- The *motive* of God's discipline is love (v. 6).
- The *goal* of God's discipline is our holiness (v. 10).
- The *present experience* of God's discipline is painful (v. 11).
- The *long-term fruit* of God's discipline is a harvest of righteousness in our lives (v. 11).

11. *We know from elsewhere in the book of Hebrews that the main form of divine discipline these believers were experiencing was persecution for their faith.*

- What are some other forms of divine discipline that you've experienced or are currently experiencing?
- How can this passage's teaching help you grow through these trials of faith?
- What fruit of God's discipline have you seen in your own life? What encouragement does this provide as you experience God's discipline now?

12. *As we considered at the outset of this study, some people consider the very idea of church discipline—drawing attention to others' sin, calling for repentance, and so on—to be mean spirited and hateful. How would you respond to someone who held this view in light of what we've seen in this passage?*

WEEK 2
FORMATIVE DISCIPLINE: BUILDING UP THE CHURCH

GETTING STARTED

Thankfully, most of the discipline we experience in our daily lives is of the formative variety. That is, all of us do things that, while they may not always be fun or exciting, help us to develop and grow in a variety of ways.

1. What are some positive examples of this kind of formative discipline in your daily life?

MAIN IDEA

God calls all the members of a local church to build each other up in love so that the church will grow in holiness. That is, he calls all of us to practice formative discipline with one another: to encourage and instruct one another in living as Christians.

DIGGING IN

As we saw in the previous study, theologians call this corporate building up "formative discipline," because it is the means by which church members help each other grow to maturity in Christ.

In Colossians 3, the apostle Paul instructs us about how we are to do this:

> [12] Put on then, as God's chosen ones, holy and beloved, compassionate hearts, kindness, humility, meekness, and patience, [13] bearing with one another and, if one has a complaint against another, forgiving each other; as the Lord has forgiven you, so you also must forgive. [14] And above all these put on love, which binds everything together in perfect harmony. [15] And let the peace of Christ rule in

your hearts, to which indeed you were called in one body. And be thankful. ¹⁶ Let the word of Christ dwell in you richly, teaching and admonishing one another in all wisdom, singing psalms and hymns and spiritual songs, with thankfulness in your hearts to God. ¹⁷ And whatever you do, in word or deed, do everything in the name of the Lord Jesus, giving thanks to God the Father through him. (vv. 12–17)

1. What does Paul tell us to "put on" in verses 12 through 14?

2. What does it mean to "put on" a compassionate heart, or humility, or love? (Hint: For context, look back at what Paul has said to "put to death" and "put away" in verses 5 through 11.)

3. What are our motivations to "put on" all these things? How do these help us to do each of them (vv. 12–14)?

4. Why does Paul say that we are to put on love "above all these"? What's unique about love (v. 14)?

5. Which of the things that Paul says to put on do you struggle with the most? Why? What are some steps you can take to grow in this area? (Hint: Ask people in the group if they have any ideas!)

6. What do all of the specific actions Paul exhorts us to do in verses 12 through 16 have in common? What does this teach us about how we are to grow spiritually?

7. What are we to let rule in our hearts (v. 15)? Why (v. 15)? What effect will this have on our relationships in the local church?

8. What does Paul say we are to do with the word of Christ? What specific examples does he give of how we are to do this (v. 16)?

9. How does singing psalms, hymns, and spiritual songs help us grow to maturity in Christ?

10. How is it that singing *is part of how we teach and admonish one another? In view of this, how should we approach our church's times of corporate praise?*

11. *What are some concrete ways you can teach, admonish, and encourage others this week?*

12. *What are some ways you regularly try to grow as an individual Christian? How can you harness those ways to help others grow as well?*

WEEK 3
DEALING WITH SIN, PART 1

GETTING STARTED

1. Have you ever had a serious medical operation? How did it feel at the time? What were the longer-term effects?

2. What might have happened to you if you didn't have that operation?

In some ways, confronting sin in others' lives—what we've referred to as corrective discipline—is like surgery. It's painful. It takes a skillful hand. No one looks forward to it. Yet the health of the whole church requires it. And when we obey God and discipline one another in this way, it can bring great blessing for everyone involved.

MAIN IDEA

God calls us to lovingly confront and restore our fellow church members who are caught in sin.

DIGGING IN

In Galatians 5, Paul points to the freedom we have in Christ and the power we have in the Spirit to obey God. In Galatians 6, he explains how we are to deal with each other's sin in the church.

> [1] Brothers, if anyone is caught in any transgression, you who are spiritual should restore him in a spirit of gentleness. Keep watch on yourself, lest you too be tempted. [2] Bear one another's burdens, and so fulfill the law of Christ. [3] For if anyone thinks he is something, when he is nothing, he deceives himself. [4] But let each one test his own work, and then his reason to boast will be in himself alone and not in his neighbor. [5] For each will have to bear his own load. (Gal. 6:1–5)

GUARDING ONE ANOTHER

1. Do you think Paul's instructions here were just for one specific situation in the churches he was writing to, or are they general guidelines for the church's life? Explain your answer from the text. (See especially verse 1.)

2. Who does Paul say should do something when someone is caught in a transgression (v. 1)?

3. Read Galatians 5:16–25. According to Paul's teaching earlier in Galatians, what does it mean to be "spiritual"?

4. What responsibility does Paul give to those who are spiritual (v. 1)? Why is this important for the health of the church?

5. In what spirit are we to restore those who sin (v. 1)?

   a) What is the opposite of this kind of spirit? Give practical examples.
   b) Why is it important to restore someone in this kind of spirit?

6. Practically speaking, what steps are involved in restoring someone who is caught in sin?

7. What does Paul tell those who are restoring another to do for themselves (v. 1)? Why do you think that this kind of work could lead to temptation?

8. What does Paul instruct us to do for one another in verse 2? What do we accomplish by doing this (v. 2)?

9. What are some burdens other members of your church bear? What are practical ways you can help to bear them?

10. What does Paul tell us to do with respect to ourselves (v. 4)?

   a) For what purpose (v. 4)?
   b) Why is this necessary (v. 5)?
   c) What does it mean that we will each have to bear our own load?
   d) How does this fit with what Paul says earlier about how we are to bear each other's burdens?

11. Do you think that Paul's teaching in this passage means that we have to rebuke someone every time they ever commit a sin? Why or why not? (See 1 Pet. 4:8.)

12. What are some obstacles that get in the way of our caring for one another in this way? By God's grace, how can you seek to overcome them? Give specific examples.

WEEK 4
DEALING WITH SIN, PART 2

GETTING STARTED

In this lesson we come to a touchy subject: excluding someone from the church because they refuse to repent of their sin.

Yet in his book *Stop Dating the Church*, Josh Harris suggests that we should actually be *excited* about the possibility of being excluded from the church. Why on earth would he say that? Harris explains,

> I gain a wonderful sense of protection in knowing that if I committed a scandalous sin and showed no repentance, my church wouldn't put up with it. They would plead with me to change. They would patiently confront me with God's Word. And eventually, if I refused to change, they would lovingly kick me out.[1]

1. What do you think about the idea that someone could be excluded from the church?

MAIN IDEA

Jesus teaches us to deal with sin in the church by confronting those who sin and exhorting them to repent. If the person doesn't repent even after being confronted by two or three others and then the whole church, the church is to exclude that person from its membership.

DIGGING IN

In Matthew 18, Jesus teaches us to become like children in order to enter God's kingdom (vv. 1–6), to not cause any others in the church to sin (vv. 7–9), and to rejoice with God over those who repent of sin

---

[1]Joshua Harris, *Stop Dating the Church!: Fall in Love with the Family of God* (Colorado Springs, CO: Multnomah, 2004), 94.

(vv. 10–14). In verse 15, he tells us how to respond if a fellow church member sins against us:

> ¹⁵ If your brother sins against you, go and tell him his fault, between you and him alone. If he listens to you, you have gained your brother. ¹⁶ But if he does not listen, take one or two others along with you, that every charge may be established by the evidence of two or three witnesses. ¹⁷ If he refuses to listen to them, tell it to the church. And if he refuses to listen even to the church, let him be to you as a Gentile and a tax collector. ¹⁸ Truly, I say to you, whatever you bind on earth shall be bound in heaven, and whatever you loose on earth shall be loosed in heaven. ¹⁹ Again I say to you, if two of you agree on earth about anything they ask, it will be done for them by my Father in heaven. ²⁰ For where two or three are gathered in my name, there am I among them. (Matt. 18:15–20)

1. How should we respond when a fellow Christian sins against us (v. 15)?

2. What's the goal of this confrontation (v. 15)?

3. What would it mean for the person to "listen to you" (v. 15)? How should you treat someone who repents of their sin when you confront them?

4. What does Jesus say we are to do if the person does not listen and repent (v. 16)?

5. What kind of people do you think you should involve at this stage in the process?

6. What does Jesus say to do if the person does not listen to the two or three others you bring along with you (v. 17)?

7. In verse 17, Jesus says, "And if he refuses to listen even to the church. . . ."
—what does this teach us about what the church is to do in this situation?

8. What does Jesus say the church is to do if the person does not listen even to the church (v. 17)?

9. What does this teach us about who has the final responsibility in matters of church discipline?

Traditionally, this step in the process of church discipline has been called "excommunication." Since communion, or the Lord's Supper, is the visible sign of someone's ongoing participation in the fellowship and membership of the church, to be excluded from membership is to be excluded from communion.

Thus, in a situation in which an individual does not repent after being confronted privately, by two or three others, and by the whole church, Jesus instructs the church to exclude that person from the membership and fellowship of the church. They are no longer to regard the individual as a brother or sister, but as an outsider.

10. After an unrepentant individual has been excluded from the church, what should you do if:

    a) The person contacts you and wants to hang out?
    b) The person is a close friend of yours?
    c) The person is a family member of yours?

11. Do you think Jesus means for us to go through this process for any sin anyone ever commits?

The point of Jesus's teaching in this passage is not that we must be perfect or else we'll be kicked out of the church, but that we must continually repent of sin. Even as Christians, we still sin in many ways (James 3:2)—the question is, what do we do about it?

12. What are some practical steps you can take to help ensure that you and other members of your church continually repent of sin?

WEEK 5
DEALING WITH SIN, PART 3

GETTING STARTED

1. *What would you do if you discovered that a member of your church was committing a sin so serious it would even scandalize non-Christians in your community?*

MAIN IDEA

If a professing Christian's sin is so serious that it renders his or her claim to be a Christian no longer believable, the church should exclude that person from their membership and not associate with him or her until it can observe the fruits of repentance.

DIGGING IN

After addressing the Corinthians' division-causing attitudes toward church leaders in the first four chapters of 1 Corinthians, in chapter 5 Paul takes on a massive moral failure on the part of the whole church. He writes,

[1] It is actually reported that there is sexual immorality among you, and of a kind that is not tolerated even among pagans, for a man has his father's wife. [2] And you are arrogant! Ought you not rather to mourn? Let him who has done this be removed from among you.

[3] For though absent in body, I am present in spirit; and as if present, I have already pronounced judgment on the one who did such a thing. [4] When you are assembled in the name of the Lord Jesus and my spirit is present, with the power of our Lord Jesus, [5] you are to deliver this man to Satan for the destruction of the flesh, so that his spirit may be saved in the day of the Lord.

[6] Your boasting is not good. Do you not know that a little leaven leavens the whole lump? [7] Cleanse out the old leaven that you may be a new lump, as you really are unleavened. For Christ, our Passover

lamb, has been sacrificed. [8] Let us therefore celebrate the festival, not with the old leaven, the leaven of malice and evil, but with the unleavened bread of sincerity and truth.

[9] I wrote to you in my letter not to associate with sexually immoral people— [10] not at all meaning the sexually immoral of this world, or the greedy and swindlers, or idolaters, since then you would need to go out of the world. [11] But now I am writing to you not to associate with anyone who bears the name of brother if he is guilty of sexual immorality or greed, or is an idolater, reviler, drunkard, or swindler—not even to eat with such a one. [12] For what have I to do with judging outsiders? Is it not those inside the church whom you are to judge? [13] God judges those outside. "Purge the evil person from among you." (1 Cor. 5:1–13)

1. *What is reported to be occurring in the Corinthian church (v. 1)?*

2. *What is the Corinthians' attitude toward this behavior (v. 2)?*

3. *What is Paul's attitude toward this behavior (vv. 2, 5)?*

4. *What does Paul tell the Corinthians to do about this (vv. 2–5)?*

5. *With regard to the immoral man, what's the goal of this act of church discipline (v. 5)?*

What does Paul mean when he commands the church to "deliver this man to Satan for the destruction of the flesh"? Simply that in being put out of the church's fellowship, the man would be, as it were, back in Satan's kingdom, the sphere where Satan rules. And the goal of this exclusion, as we've seen, is that this judgment by the church would cause the man to come to his senses, repent of his sin, and show himself to be a genuine disciple of Christ in the end.

6. *What does Paul say will happen if the church fails to address this sin? What metaphor does he appeal to? What does this teach us about sin in the church (v. 6)?*

7. What practical actions can you take to keep sin from spreading through the church?

8. What action does Paul call the Corinthians to in verses 9 and 11? What misconception does he correct in verse 10?

9. Why do you think Paul gives opposite instructions regarding how the Corinthians are to treat an immoral person who does not claim to be a Christian and one who does?

10. Whom does Paul say that the church is to judge (v. 12)?

   a) What practical action does this require (v. 13)?
   b) Do you think a church can fulfill this command if it does not formally practice church membership?

What should this look like practically?

- Just as we considered in our last study, the fact that the church is to "purge the evil person" from its midst does *not* typically mean that such an individual should be prohibited from attending church.
- It *does* mean that the individual should be removed from the church's membership and instructed not to partake in the Lord's Supper.
- It also means that members of the church should not continue to have Christian fellowship with this individual or interact with them in a casual, friendly way.

11. How does this passage differ from Jesus's teaching in Matthew 18, which we considered in the previous study (see Matt. 18:15–20)?

   a) How would you describe the major difference between the situation which prompts a "Matthew 18" response and the situation which prompts a "1 Corinthians 5" response?
   b) What are the different actions which the two passages require the church to take?

In this passage, there are a number of reasons Paul gives for why the church should exclude from its membership someone who claims to be a Christian but lives in gross immorality.

First, it's good for the person who is excluded. Someone who claims to be a Christian but lives in immorality is deceiving themselves. They need a loud, clear reminder that those who live in that way will not inherit the kingdom of God (1 Cor. 6:9–10). It is a loving act, therefore, to exclude such an individual from the church in the hope that it will lead them to repentance (v. 5).

Second, it's good for the church. As Paul explains in verses 6 through 8, sin is like leaven, or yeast: it keeps spreading until it permeates the whole church. In order for the church to be pure and holy as God calls it to be, the church must cut off someone whose life is characterized by sin.

Third, it's good for the world. How? Because a church that is marked by godliness portrays a vivid, compelling picture of the gospel to the world. But a church that is filled with people who live just like the world broadcasts the lie that God isn't holy, that he doesn't care about how we live, and that the good news about Jesus doesn't really have power to transform our lives. Christians bear God's name before the world, so our conduct must reflect God's character, not the ways of this world (vv. 1, 11).

12. In light of the things we've seen in this passage, how would you explain church discipline to someone who thought that it was mean, exclusive, and unloving?

WEEK 6
REPENTANCE AND
RESTORATION

GETTING STARTED

1. Have you ever confronted a fellow Christian about sin in his or her life? What was your goal in doing this? How did it go?

MAIN IDEA

With respect to the disciplined individual, the goal of church discipline is to help the individual repent of sin and be restored to fellowship in the church.

DIGGING IN

The past few studies have focused on how we are to address sin within the church, including excluding someone from the church if they persist in serious, unrepentant sin. In this study we're going to consider the goal of these actions, namely that the individual would repent and be restored to the church.

Paul writes in 2 Corinthians 2:

> [5] Now if anyone has caused pain, he has caused it not to me, but in some measure—not to put it too severely—to all of you. [6] For such a one, this punishment by the majority is enough, [7] so you should rather turn to forgive and comfort him, or he may be overwhelmed by excessive sorrow. [8] So I beg you to reaffirm your love for him. [9] For this is why I wrote, that I might test you and know whether you are obedient in everything. [10] Anyone whom you forgive, I also forgive. Indeed, what I have forgiven, if I have forgiven anything, has been for your sake in the presence of Christ, [11] so that we would not be outwitted by Satan; for we are not ignorant of his designs. (2 Cor. 2:5–11)

Note: While many interpreters have identified the individual in this passage with the man Paul refers to in 1 Corinthians 5, it seems best to see these passages as referring to different people. There are several reasons for this, but one of the strongest is that it is extremely unlikely that Paul would have downplayed the sin the way he does in this passage ("Indeed, what I have forgiven, *if I have forgiven anything.* . . .") if he were referring to the man who had his father's wife.

Instead, from what we learn in the rest of the letter, it seems that this incident had to do with someone stirring up opposition to Paul among the Corinthians. That explains why he graciously downplays the seriousness of the sin in question.

1. What action has the Corinthian church already taken (v. 6)?

2. In light of verse 7 and the teaching we've examined in the past few studies, what form do you think this "punishment" took?

3. What does Paul tell the Corinthian church to do now (vv. 7–8)?

4. What are the reasons Paul tells them to do this (vv. 6–7)? What does Paul not want to happen?

5. What does it mean that the church is to reaffirm their love for this man?

6. What would it practically look like for your church to reaffirm their love for someone who had been excluded? Give specific examples.

7. Based on this passage, under what circumstances should a church accept someone who's been excluded back into their fellowship? When should a church not accept someone back?

That a church should accept back an individual if they repent of their sin—and only if they repent—naturally leads us to ask, "What does true repentance look like?" We learn something about this in 2 Corinthians 7, in which Paul draws attention to how the

Corinthians themselves repented over their former toleration of this man who opposed Paul:

> [5] For even when we came into Macedonia, our bodies had no rest, but we were afflicted at every turn—fighting without and fear within. [6] But God, who comforts the downcast, comforted us by the coming of Titus, [7] and not only by his coming but also by the comfort with which he was comforted by you, as he told us of your longing, your mourning, your zeal for me, so that I rejoiced still more. [8] For even if I made you grieve with my letter, I do not regret it—though I did regret it, for I see that that letter grieved you, though only for a while. [9] As it is, I rejoice, not because you were grieved, but because you were grieved into repenting. For you felt a godly grief, so that you suffered no loss through us.
> [10] For godly grief produces a repentance that leads to salvation without regret, whereas worldly grief produces death. [11] For see what earnestness this godly grief has produced in you, but also what eagerness to clear yourselves, what indignation, what fear, what longing, what zeal, what punishment! At every point you have proved yourselves innocent in the matter. [12] So although I wrote to you, it was not for the sake of the one who did the wrong, nor for the sake of the one who suffered the wrong, but in order that your earnestness for us might be revealed to you in the sight of God. [13] Therefore we are comforted. (2 Cor. 7:5–13)

Apparently, Paul wrote another letter to the Corinthians that hasn't been preserved. It seems that in this letter, Paul strongly rebuked the church for embracing someone who opposed him and sought to undercut his ministry, and he instructed the church to exclude him from their midst. This explains why Paul was waiting anxiously to hear how the Corinthian church received his letter (7:5–7) and why Paul can say that their response to his letter revealed their earnestness *for him* (7:13).

8. Did Paul regret that he wrote to the Corinthians? Why or why not (v. 8)?

9. Does Paul regret that he wrote to the Corinthians? Why or why not (vv. 8–9)?

10. What can pastors and other church leaders learn from Paul's attitude and actions toward the Corinthians?

11. What does worldly grief produce? What does godly grief produce (vv. 10–11)? Give some real-life examples of both, whether from the Bible or your own experience.

12. Imagine that a person has committed a serious sin and it's come to light. This sin is so serious that the church has excluded the person from their membership. It's now a couple months later, and the person feels terrible about it all.

How do you think the church could assess whether the person has genuinely repented or is merely experiencing worldly grief? What are some factors that should go into making this judgment?

TEACHER'S NOTES FOR WEEK 1

DIGGING IN

1. In verse 3, the author exhorts us to consider him who endured such hostility from sinners against himself (that is, Jesus). Why? So that we would not grow weary or fainthearted. This passage is one indication among many others in Hebrews that the believers who received this letter were being violently persecuted for their faith. This experience of persecution and suffering for the faith forms the backdrop for the rest of this passage.

2. The exhortation of verses 5 and 6 addresses us as *sons*. This teaches us that God's attitude toward us is that of a wise, loving, generous father.

3. We can be sure that God's fatherly discipline of his children is always done lovingly and for his children's good. It can be painful, as we'll consider in a moment, but we can trust that it's being done by a loving, tender, and good heavenly father—our less-than-perfect experience with earthly fathers notwithstanding.

4. The exhortation of verses 5 and 6 tells us, in two sets of parallel phrases, not to despise or be weary with God's discipline because God disciplines every child whom he loves. That is, God teaches, trains, rebukes, and chastises us—often by providentially ordering various trials of our faith—for our ultimate good.

5. One reason it would be especially comforting to know that persecution (or any other painful circumstance) is God's fatherly work of discipline is that during a trial it could be tempting to think that God is abandoning us. It could be tempting to think that God is angry with us or has withdrawn from us, when in fact exactly the opposite is true. Meditating on this truth can help us transform our mind-set regarding trials. The better we understand that trials are designed by God to draw us closer to him, the better we will be prepared to glorify God through steadfastly trusting God and depending on him.

6. Verses 7 through 11 draw a comparison between the way God disciplines us and the way that earthly fathers discipline their children. This helps us to understand God's discipline better in that most of us have some experience of our earthly fathers—however imperfectly—disciplining us and teaching us for our good.

7. Verse 8 says that those whom God does not discipline are illegitimate children and not sons of God. This should comfort us when we experience

God's discipline because it teaches us that being disciplined by God is a mark of a true child of God. This reminds us of God's love for us and of the rich inheritance he has stored up for us, his children.

8. The proper response to parental discipline, which the author assumes his readers would all recognize, is respect and the obedience that flows from respect.

9. According to verse 10, our earthly fathers disciplined us:

- *for a short time*
- as it *seemed* best *to them.*

But God disciplines us:

- *for our good*
- *that we may share his holiness.*

This teaches us that we should submit ourselves to God as he disciplines us. Since we respected our earthly parents who disciplined us imperfectly, according to what seemed best to them, how much more should we submit to the all-powerful Creator and Lord of the universe, who always disciplines us for our good and who knows perfectly what is ultimately best for us?

10. *Now* discipline is painful, but *later*, once we've been trained by it, it yields a harvest of "the peaceful fruit of righteousness" in our lives. Concrete examples given will vary, but they can include just about anything!

11. Answers will vary.

12. Answers will vary, but the basic idea is that discipline is actually loving because it has as its aim every church member's holiness, which will be for their eternal good.

TEACHER'S NOTES FOR WEEK 2

DIGGING IN

1. In verses 12 through 14 Paul tells us to "put on" compassionate hearts, kindness, humility, meekness, patience, and love, as well as to bear with one another and to forgive each other.

2. To "put on" a compassionate heart, kindness, and so on is to deliberately, purposefully strive to live in those ways. Even as those who are being renewed in Christ's image, these things do not come naturally or effortlessly, since sin still lives within us. Thus Paul calls us to work to cultivate these godly, gospel-driven virtues.

3. First, we are to put on these things as God's chosen ones, those who are holy and beloved (v. 12). This motivates us to pursue holiness in that we know God loves us and has chosen us despite our sin. The fact that we *are* holy motivates us to pursue these virtues because they are in accordance with who God has already made us to be in Christ. Second, we are to forgive each other as we have been forgiven (v. 13). This reminds us that if God has forgiven the massive debt of our sin, we should be willing and able to forgive others' comparatively minor offenses against us. See Jesus's parable in Matthew 18:21–35 for a vivid illustration of this.

4. Paul says to put on love "above all these" because love is what binds all of these other virtues together in perfect harmony (v. 14). Love is the overarching posture which we must have if we are to be genuinely compassionate, kind, humble, meek, and so on, and love ties all of these things together into a harmonious whole.

5. Answers will vary.

6. What all of Paul's specific instructions in verses 12 through 16 have in common is that they all relate to how we interact with others. None of them are individualistic. They all bear on relationships in the local church. This teaches us that spiritual growth doesn't happen just between us and Jesus, as we read the Bible alone in our room. Rather, true spiritual growth involves a whole web of relationships in a local church in which we help others to grow and they in turn help us to grow. Further, one of the main tests of our maturity in Christ is how we relate to others within the body of Christ.

7. We are to let the peace of Christ rule in our hearts (v. 15). Why? Because we were called in that peace to one body. If we do allow Christ's peace to rule

in our hearts, it will make us peacemakers in the body of Christ, seeking others' good and counting them more important than ourselves.

8. In verse 16, Paul says that we are to let the word of Christ dwell in us richly. The specific ways we are to do this are teaching and admonishing one another and singing songs, hymns, and spiritual songs.

9. Singing psalms, hymns, and spiritual songs helps us grow to maturity in Christ because it engages our minds and hearts with the truths of the gospel in a way that makes a vivid impression on us. It unites our intellects and affections and infuses both with gospel truth in a way that shapes our characters around the truths of the gospel.

10. Singing is part of how we teach and admonish one another in that our singing is addressed not only to God, but also to each other. As we worship God, we also encourage each other with the truth about who God is and what he's done. In view of this, we should approach our church's times of corporate praise with our attention first on God, but also on each other as we consider how we can encourage and admonish each other. This means that the goal of the church's time of corporate singing is not that each of us would have a sensational emotional experience but that we would glorify God, build up each other, and have our own hearts instructed in the truth.

11–12. Answers will vary.

TEACHER'S NOTES FOR WEEK 3

DIGGING IN

1. Paul's instructions in verse 1 are applicable to all Christians in all churches. He's *not* writing about a specific situation because he says, "If *anyone* is caught in *any* transgression. . ." (v. 1).

2. Paul says that those "who are spiritual" are to do something about this (v. 1).

3. As we see from the immediately preceding passage, Galatians 5:16–25, by "spiritual" Paul means someone who has the Spirit of God dwelling in them and who therefore strives against their flesh to do what God commands. In a sense, Paul's term "spiritual" could refer to all Christians (and it sometimes does), but in this context he probably means something more specific such as "those of you who are spiritually mature" or "those of you who are walking more in step with the Spirit," since the contrast is with someone who is caught in sin.

4. Paul gives those who are spiritual the responsibility to restore the sinning Christian in a spirit of gentleness (v. 1). This is important for the health of the church because if sin goes unchecked, it will spread through the whole body. In 1 Corinthians 5:6, Paul says, "Do you not know that a little leaven leavens the whole lump?" and then goes on to exhort the Corinthians to deal properly with the sin in their midst. The health of the church depends on our ability to deal rightly with sin, because we all still struggle with sin and we need all the help we can get!

5. Paul says that those who are spiritual are to restore such a one *in a spirit of gentleness* (v. 1).

   a) The opposite of this kind of spirit is a harsh, judgmental attitude which seeks to inflict more guilt on the sinner rather than pointing them to God's grace in Christ.
   b) It's important to restore someone in this kind of spirit for a number of reasons:
      • First, as we confront someone else's sin, it's important for us to recognize that we are sinners, too, and that everything we have is from God's grace. If we don't recognize this and cultivate a spirit of gentleness as a result, we may become puffed up with pride and self-righteousness.

- Second, it's important to have a gentle spirit because no one likes to be confronted. When someone points out your sin, it's easy to become defensive or even angry. Thus, the one who would correct another's sin must do so as kindly and patiently as possible, being ready to defuse conflict rather than pour gasoline on the fire.

6. Practically speaking, restoring someone who's caught in sin involves:

- Confronting the person's sin, bringing it to their attention, and reminding them from Scripture why it is wrong.
- Reminding the person of the gospel, the good news that through Christ's substitutionary death on our behalf, God counts us as completely righteous in his sight and forgives *all* our sins through faith in Christ.
- Reminding the person that through what Christ has done for us, we now have the Holy Spirit dwelling within us who enables us to live lives that are pleasing to God. It's important to remind people of this so that they would not despair in their sin but take hope that by God's power they can overcome it.
- Providing whatever practical help and encouragement to help the person overcome this sin in the future.
- Helping the person to work through reconciliation with others or restitution for wrongs committed if need be.

7. Paul tells those who are restoring another to "keep watch on yourself, lest you too be tempted" (v. 1). Those doing such work could be tempted to fall into the sin they are trying to pull someone out of, or a sin such as pride or self-righteousness could arise if we consider ourselves better than the one we're restoring.

8. In verse 2, Paul instructs us to bear one another's burdens. By doing so, we fulfill the law of Christ.

9. Answers will vary.

10. Concerning ourselves, Paul tells each of us to test our own work.

a) He tells us to do this so that we would have reason to boast in ourselves and not in another (vv. 4–5). Does this mean that Paul wants us to derive a kind of self-righteous satisfaction from the good that we do? Not at all! (See 1 Cor. 4:7.) But it does mean that each of us should have confidence before God that we are walking in his ways,

and the way we develop that confidence is through disciplined
self-examination.

b) This is necessary because each of us will bear his own load (v. 5).

c) This means that each of us will give an account to God and will
answer to him for how we have lived.

d) To bear one another's burdens is to help each other in our weak-
nesses, sins, and infirmities. That we will each have to bear our own
load on the last day means that we are all finally accountable to God.
These do not contradict each other. Rather, these two statements
show that we both need other people to help us and depend on others
in the Christian life, and that we are finally accountable to God for
how we live.

11. Paul's teaching in this passage doesn't mean that we should rebuke
someone every time they ever sin. That would be both ridiculous and
impossible. Rather, as Peter tells us, "Love covers over a multitude of sins,"
(1 Pet. 4:8). And as Paul says elsewhere, we are to patiently bear with one
another and forgive each other (Eph. 4:32). Thus, discernment is required
in order to determine when you need to confront someone's sin and when
you should simply pass over it in love. The scenario Paul has in mind in this
passage seems to involve more serious sin, since Paul describes an individual as being caught in it or overtaken by it.

12. Answers will vary.

TEACHER'S NOTES FOR WEEK 4

DIGGING IN

1. When someone sins against us, Jesus instructs us to go and tell him his fault privately (v. 15).

2. The goal of this confrontation is that the individual would repent and the relationship would be healed (v. 15). That's what Jesus means when he says, "If he listens to you, you have gained your brother."

3. If the person "listens," that means that he or she acknowledge his or her sin and repent of it. If the person does repent, we should reextend full, loving Christian fellowship. Jesus says, "If he listens to you, you have gained your brother," which means that we have won him back from his sin and so should affirm him in Christ. We should *not* hold his sin over his head or try to make him feel guilty for it.

4. Jesus says that if the person doesn't repent, we should bring two or three others with us to appeal to the person again (v. 16).

5. At this stage in the process you should involve mature, godly believers. You should involve people who can speak gently, biblically, and soberly. Depending on the seriousness of the sin, you should begin to involve your church's elders either at this point or very soon after.

6. Jesus says that if the person doesn't listen to the two or three others we bring along with us, we are to tell it to the church (v. 17). In light of the elders' responsibility to lead and shepherd the church, it is probably best for the elders to be the ones to actually present the matter to the church. And given the sensitive nature of the matter, as well as Jesus's implicit instruction to keep the matter as private as possible at each stage, it would be best to communicate to the church about this in a meeting that consists entirely of the church's members rather than a meeting that includes visitors as well.

7. The fact that Jesus says "if he refuses to listen even to the church" indicates that the church as a whole is to plead with the person to repent. At the very least this means that the church's leaders should engage the individual, and anyone who has a personal relationship with the person should plead with him or her to repent of the sin.

8. Jesus says that if the person doesn't repent, the church as a whole is to treat the person as a Gentile and a tax collector (v. 17). That is, the church is to exclude the person from its membership. This doesn't mean that the individual should be excluded from the church's public meetings. In fact,

in most circumstances, the person should be encouraged to continue to sit under the preaching of the Word in the hope that he or she will be convicted of the sin and will repent. Yet the individual should be removed from the church's membership and instructed not to participate in the Lord's Supper until he or she repents of the sin and is accepted back into membership by the church.

9. That Jesus addresses the whole church in this way indicates that the congregation as a whole has the final authority over matters of church discipline. Thus, while the church's elders should exercise significant leadership throughout this process, the church as a whole must decide to exclude the individual from membership.

10. a) If the excluded individual contacts you and wants to hang out, you should decline his or her invitation and exhort that person to repent of this sin and be reconciled to God.

  b) If the person is a close friend of yours, the same thing goes. You should convey to that person that while you still love and desire what's best for him or her, you are not going to spend time together or continue as friends in the same manner unless and until the person repents.

  c) If the person who is excluded from the church is a family member of yours, the situation is more complicated. Since you are family, you have a biblical obligation to interact with and maintain a relationship with the person that is independent of his or her membership in the church. Thus, you should continue to interact with the person as a loving, caring family member. Yet your interactions with the individual should reflect the fact that he or she must repent of this sin and be reconciled to God.

11. Jesus clearly doesn't mean for us to go through this process with every sin a person ever commits because 1 Peter tells us that love covers over a multitude of sins (1 Pet. 4:8). We should go through this process when a person's sin is outward (a matter of actions or words, not merely internal attitudes), serious, and unrepentant. Inevitably this will require discernment.

12. Answers will vary.

TEACHER'S NOTES FOR WEEK 5

DIGGING IN

1. It is reported that there is a man in the church at Corinth who is in a sexual relationship with his father's wife, presumably his stepmother (v. 1).

2. The Corinthians' attitude toward this man's behavior is boastful tolerance (v. 2). Paul calls them "arrogant" about the matter, suggesting that they were taking pride in their own toleration of this sin.

3. Paul's attitude toward this behavior is that it is utterly deplorable and worthy of God's judgment. In fact, he says in verse 3 that he himself has already passed judgment on the man.

4. Paul tells the Corinthians that they are to mourn over this man's sin and remove him from among them (v. 2). Paul further describes this act as handing the man over to Satan (vv. 4–5). What does this mean practically? They were to exclude him from their fellowship and no longer associate with him as a brother.

5. With regard to the man himself, the goal of church discipline is that it would lead to his sinful nature being destroyed and his spirit being saved on the day of Christ (v. 5). The goal is that the church's act of excluding the man from their fellowship would result in his repenting of this sin, turning to Christ for mercy, and beginning to live in a way that demonstrates genuine repentance and faith in Christ.

6. Paul warns that if the church fails to address this sin, it will "leaven" the whole church—that is, sin will spread through the whole church like yeast through dough (v. 6). The image Paul is appealing to is that a little leaven or yeast spreads through a whole lump of dough until it permeates the dough completely. This teaches us that sin is viral and contagious. If left unaddressed, it spreads through a church until it infects the whole.

7. Answers will vary.

8. In verses 9 and 11, Paul calls the church not to associate with anyone who "bears the name of brother," that is, claims to be a Christian, but who lives in immorality. The misconception he corrects is that apparently, when he wrote to the Corinthians about this previously, they mistook him to mean that they shouldn't associate with people of the world who are immoral. That is, they thought Paul meant for them to separate from immoral people who didn't claim to be Christians. But Paul only meant that they were

not to associate with anyone who "bears the name of brother" yet lives in immorality.

9. Paul gives opposite instructions about how the Corinthians are to interact with immoral non-Christians and immoral professing Christians because he only expects Christians to live like Christians!

It's also clear that Paul is concerned about the church's corporate testimony before the world. It is the person who "bears the name of brother" who is to be excluded from the church if he persists in serious immorality. Paul exhorts the church to separate from such people because if we don't, we give the impression that this way of living is consistent with being a Christian. If Christians live like non-Christians, our actions lie about who Jesus is and what he came to do.

10. Paul says that the church is to judge those who are inside the church, not those who are outside (v. 12).

   a) This requires us, in Paul's words, to "purge the evil person" from among us (v. 13).
   b) Can a church faithfully carry this out without formally practicing church membership? No. Without some public means of identifying those who do and do not belong to the church, there's no way for the church to know who is "inside" and who is "outside."

11. This passage differs from Jesus's teaching in Matthew 18:15–20 in the kind of sin it addresses and the kind of response it calls for from the church.

   a) *Nature of the sin*: In Matthew 18, the sin in question is a matter of one believer sinning against another. It also seems to be relevant to other kinds of sins a church member might commit which, if not let go of, *eventually* render the person's profession unbelievable. In 1 Corinthians 5, the matter is a seriously scandalous sin that is apparently known to the whole church. It's the kind of sin that *immediately* renders a person's profession unbelievable.
   b) *The nature of the church's response*: Matthew 18 calls for a slow, incremental broadening of the number of people involved. The goal is to bring the person to repentance using as few people as possible. First Corinthians 5 calls the church to exclude the individual immediately due to the seriousness of the sin.

12. Answers will vary.

TEACHER'S NOTES FOR WEEK 6

DIGGING IN

1. The Corinthian church, through a decision by "the majority," has "punished" the man who did this sinful act that "caused pain" to Paul and to the church.

2. Verse 7 urges the church to reaffirm their love for this man and forgive him, which means that the "punishment" the church delivered was excluding this man from their fellowship because of his sin. This is confirmed by Matthew 18:15–20 and 1 Corinthians 5, the passages we've considered in the previous two studies, because both passages tell the church to exclude someone from their fellowship if the person's sin is so serious that it renders their profession of faith not credible.

3. Now Paul tells the Corinthian church to forgive this man, comfort him, and reaffirm their love for him (vv. 7–8).

4. Paul tells them to do this because: 1) "the punishment by the majority" is enough for him; that is to say, it has had its effect and led him to repentance, and so there is nothing more that the man should suffer; 2) so that the man does not become overwhelmed by sorrow. Paul does *not* want the church to keep on holding this man's sin over his head because he doesn't want the man's spirit to be crushed.

5. That the church is to reaffirm their love for this man means that they are to welcome him back into their membership and treat him again as a fellow Christian, bearing his burdens, encouraging him in the faith, and so on. This would likely have at least some kind of public element where the church formally extends their forgiveness, reaffirms their love for him, and welcomes him back into fellowship. Practical examples of what this would look like in a given local church will vary.

6. Answers will vary.

7. Based on Paul's teaching in this passage, it is clear that the church should accept someone back into membership if he or she repents of the sin for which they were excluded. The church should not accept someone back into membership if he or she continues to commit the same sin or otherwise fail to demonstrate true repentance.

8. Paul *did* regret that he wrote to the Corinthians because his letter made the Corinthians grieve (v. 8).

9. Paul *doesn't* regret that he wrote to the Corinthians—that is, he did regret it, but he doesn't any longer—because he sees that his letter caused them to grieve over their sin and repent of it (vv. 8–9). Now, he rejoices because they have come to see their sin for what it was, turn from it, and bear good spiritual fruit.

10. There are a number of lessons that pastors and church leaders can learn from Paul's actions and attitudes seen in these passages. Here are just a couple of them:

First, pastors can learn that they should have mercy on those who genuinely grieve for their sin, and they should be quick to lead the church to show mercy to those who genuinely repent after being excluded from the church. This doesn't necessarily mean that the church should instantly welcome back an individual as soon as he or she claims to repent (after all, Paul is also aware that there is a kind of worldly grief that isn't true repentance). It *does* mean that a pastor should have a tender, merciful posture, being eager to forgive and sensitive toward the spiritual frailty of one who has been excluded from the church and has come to repentance.

Second, pastors can learn from Paul to have a tender concern for their flocks that leads them to neither callously inflict discipline on them nor be cowards and fail to rebuke them when necessary. Paul's concern for the Corinthians was such that he hated to inflict pain on them, yet he did so when it was necessary for their spiritual health. Thus, a faithful pastor will be both tough and tender. His love for his flock, like parents' love for their children, will lead him to be zealous for their true good. This will mean doing things that they don't necessarily like, yet always in a spirit of tender, affectionate care.

11. Worldly grief produces death (v. 9). But godly sorrow produces repentance that leads to salvation without regret (v. 10). In the case of the Corinthian church, their godly sorrow led to eagerness to clear themselves by doing what was right, indignation over their sin, fear of God, zeal, and willingness to expel from their midst the one who had caused them to stumble. Specific examples will, of course, vary.

12. It's impossible to offer a perfect set of principles for discerning between worldly sorrow and true repentance, but here are some general guidelines:

- One major way to tell the difference between worldly sorrow and godly sorrow is to consider the person's attitude toward the church's act of discipline. Does the person heartily agree that the church was right to exclude him or her because of this sin, or does the person harbor bitterness and resentment?

- Another way to tell the difference is whether the person appears to be more upset about how the sin has affected himself or herself (focusing on the pain, shame, or hardship it has brought him or her), or is the person genuinely grieved to have sinned against God, harmed others, wounded the church, and brought Christ's name into disrepute?
- The difficulty and sensitivity involved in this kind of situation is one reason why a church's elders should take the lead in these matters, and why those elders must be godly, patient, humble, prayerful, Bible-soaked men.

PERSONAL NOTES

PERSONAL NOTES

PERSONAL NOTES

PERSONAL NOTES

PERSONAL NOTES

PERSONAL NOTES

PERSONAL NOTES

IX 9Marks

Building Healthy Churches

9Marks exists to equip church leaders with a biblical vision and practical resources for displaying God's glory to the nations through healthy churches.

To that end, we want to see churches characterized by these nine marks of health:

1   Expositional Preaching
2   Biblical Theology
3   A Biblical Understanding of the Gospel
4   A Biblical Understanding of Conversion
5   A Biblical Understanding of Evangelism
6   Biblical Church Membership
7   Biblical Church Discipline
8   Biblical Discipleship
9   Biblical Church Leadership

Find all our Crossway titles
and other resources at
www.9Marks.org

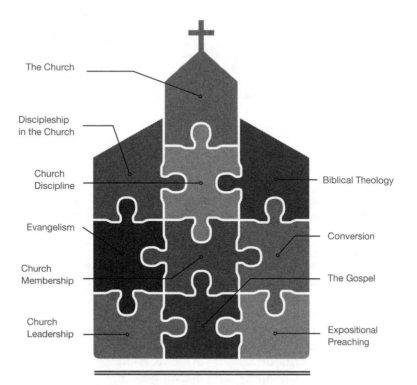

The Church
Discipleship in the Church
Church Discipline
Evangelism
Church Membership
Church Leadership
Biblical Theology
Conversion
The Gospel
Expositional Preaching

Be sure to check out the rest of the

9MARKS HEALTHY CHURCH STUDY GUIDE SERIES

This series covers the nine distinctives of a healthy church as originally laid out in *Nine Marks of a Healthy Church* by Mark Dever. Each book explores the biblical foundations of key aspects of the church, helping Christians to live out those realities as members of a local body. A perfect resource for use in Sunday school, church-wide studies, or small group contexts.